In Praise of
DEAD BOYS MAKE THE BEST MEN

Amidst loss, longing, violence, desire and dark humor in the poems of Rigel Portales lies tenderness like "[…] what light goes through." With his language and what he does and can do with it at his age to make sense of human condition and position should make us excited about what is next after *DEAD BOYS MAKE THE BEST MEN* that reminds us "What is instant/is local and lovable/ not beloved, just bled [….]"

—Vijae O. Alquisola
Teacher, Writer

In the last lines of the title-poem of this chapbook, the persona, talking to a dead friend, apparently says, "I'm having fun, writing to you…" The overall voice in this collection sounds just like that: *having fun*—with jokes, anecdotes, and vignettes, among others—playful and youthful. However, the poems in this collection are never funny; instead, they reveal an ironic seriousness in tone, filled with doubt and desire. Reading Rigel Portales's poems is akin to "hold[ing] the blade/by the blade"—you realize his poems can certainly cut deep.

— Mesándel Virtusio Arguelles
Teacher, Writer

Rigel Portales' poetry cuts incisions in the psyches of those who are lucky enough to have read and felt them. In his collection, men who kill also mourn their dead. Boys come to terms with their desire for other boys. Knives and basketballs and altar servers' frocks. The triumph of this collection is in how it carves into rage, desperation, and grief to find where love, desire, and hope are nestled. *DEAD BOYS MAKE THE BEST MEN* is an exploration of the complexities of what it means to be a man in this society, a letter of tenderness to men who have been starved of it.

— **Carlo Bautista**
Writer

DEAD BOYS MAKE THE BEST MEN

FLOWERSONG
P R E S S

a collection of poems by
Rigel Ruel Portales

FLOWERSONG
P R E S S

FlowerSong Press
Copyright © 2023 by Rigel Ruel Portales
ISBN: 978-1-953447-16-6

Published by FlowerSong Press
in the United States of America.
www.flowersongpress.com

Cover Design by Rommielle Morada
Set in Adobe Garamond Pro

NOTICE: SCHOOLS AND BUSINESSES
FlowerSong Press offers copies of this book at quantity
discount with bulk purchase for educational, business, or sales
promotional use. For information, please email the Publisher at
info@flowersongpress.com.

Table of Contents

para kay Dustin at Ricky, hindi kayo mawawala

for Dustin and Ricky, you will never disappear

DEAD BOYS
MAKE THE
BEST MEN

Dad Joke

There are some stories
that loom large as a cement truck
and some flat as a family sedan.

At lunchtime,
I watched a family of five
become a family of one.

Whoever it was that survived
was interviewed.

I decided to not
become a journalist then,
but a father.

I felt like I came to know this without question

You only turn
slightly after the corner.

My father tricks me
into saving his car
and my life.

One car-length away,
I tell you when we will veer
sharp because otherwise,
you won't give way.

When we get near, I'll reassure you.
We haven't left anything behind.
Even if we did, which we do,
which we do.

the traffic lights are out / to kill us

Each fluorescent second / seems lethally final / until the last red flicker / loses / means no bruises tonight / just tomorrow / when the green morning / threatens you / with go / get out of my fucking house / I tell you / we have done nothing / wrong / waiting / with a half-inch of grass / to kiss / around / I set my gear shift to drive / returning alive / again / took no time / again / took all our lives / surviving / beating / fastidious signals / begging us / to be hunted / the dark / slow / fastened shut / and belted glow / follow me closely / then closed.

Butterfly Knife

I felt like I had to hold the blade
by the blade. My father's side

taught me the core of a palm tree
was crying. By the fishpond. We stabbed it.

The sap crawling towards me whispered
that I wasn't bleeding yet. Mudcrabs dug

themselves in. Their claws curved forward. Proving
myself final. I pulled by the handle. Folded it

like a wing. Kept it against the artery
in my thigh.

A Country Without A Right to Carry

I imagine some guns have a life
of their own, falling into hands

that do nothing but carry
results. I imagine some live

without their hands. I imagine
some watch their life through the barrel.

Call it the moon. Watch it burn.
Then turn in its sleep.

I can't imagine millimeters
or how particular their shape is

for me to be sent to the sky.
Or the right to be

what I can't have:
A brass blanket,

A flower upon impact,
Pollen smoke.

Or what good it would do
to meet a man with a man,

praised for our caliber,
the diameter of our holes.

Blameless.

It's out of my hands

There is the boy in the barbershop who will pull me in
to the only remaining parking slot, open the door
for me, watch my keys, practice his daddy's straight razor
on my life, and midway, he will ask if I like it and I say *nothing*
looks better on me than what was prescribed.
When I am finished, he will leave to get some alcohol
for my newly-minted head. I will scratch myself under the vinyl sheet,
whisper, *it's out of my hands now,* let him massage
my cuts and pound the bevels in my back to his satisfaction.
Returning, I washed my head in the shower. On the same grounds, I prayed,
put together new words I found like leaves I meant to grow into clothes,
It made sense or *I did no wrong but remake myself*
desired. God sees through all that so I turned the lights off, let the water run
wasteful and imperceptible from these tears. God knows I am crying
and more.

Insecure Holdupper

When I scream
this is a hold-up,
I mean:
I am having second thoughts.
I am not above all this.
I'm pointing to the sky.
I insist on killing.
I'm looking out for rain.
I'm looking for counsel.
I want 37 hostages
and 37 arms
with all the threats in the world.
According to statistics,
we are God-fearing at our median.
Some passengers slip gold
into their mouths
then pray.
I draw blanks from my waistband.
I aim.
It's not too late, drop your weapon.
They brought everyone I knew
that was still alive
to mind.

I confess under my mask
that I can't do it,
never will.
I'm a virgin.
I'm a quickshot.
I give myself up to the pigs.
My farm. I want to live
until my first kiss.
A pre-loved pigsty. An empty stable.
Some animals we can house.
Some animals we can sell.
How long do I have left on this terrible earth?
The judge extended my sentence
for life, for life.

[This is what monks go through]

This is what monks go through
This is what garbagemen go through
This is what basaguleros go through
This is what light goes through

In The Last Game of 2K We Played, The Rules Stipulated That Nobody Can Stay In The Paint For Longer Than 3 Seconds

for Ricky Benig

One of these days:
I'll call him
by name
once I get it
right.
I'll call him
victim *was it?*
Or was it *tol,*
brodie?
Boasting about
how he was,
maybe I'll call him
the patron saint
of fly. Like Jordan.
Unlike Kobe
and his immaculate
fadeaways.
I'm lying I never
played basketball
once
alive
or knew if he did
when he was.
I just want us both
to fly.

One of these days, I'll call him
up. *What was his number*
on the news?
I'll leave a voicemail, a text
about how he left his
department store Nikes
homework
PS2 controller
still plugged in
at my place

Maybe
if you wanna hang out
for real,
I'll take you
on my shoulders
right now. Reach high
and push
my Spalding basketball
squeezed between the rim
and gravestone.
I'll let you free
throw for the moon,
land a wound,
then take it all the way
with you, please.

My father barges into my room and tells me he has to repair something higher than the both of us.

Son, all ladders fall
towards heaven. There is space
in your room for that.

"unverified[1] information[2] pertaining[3] to[4] alleged[5] cases[6] of[7] self[8]-[9]harm[10]"

"All this was plain to you / When you destroyed a torturable body." —Bertolt Brecht

---

[1]*unverified:* "Good evening please don't share the suicide FB news because that's not true. We know everyone is having a hard time but spreading fake news will not help. Remove your post please."

This comes from what looks like a professor.

[2]*information:* "I am an instructor and not a teacher."

This comes from what looks like a teacher.

[3]*pertaining:* "I attended the forum about Mental health last Oct 22 not knowing that on Oct 11, someone took her own life."

This comes from a student.

[4]*to:* "It was only 3 weeks after her passing that a staff member posted 'suicide is not the solution.'"

This comes from a student.

[5]*alleged:* "5 have been confirmed. 3 have yet to be confirmed. 2 are still unidentified."

This comes from a student

⁶cases: "One of the victims of suicide was a former student of mine. It appears there were 9 others in a span of a month."

This comes from a professor

⁷of: "Don't turn a blind eye towards the reason why you exist. Don't underestimate the minds of our youth."

This comes from a professor.

⁸self: "You have the option not to enroll."

This comes from a different generation.

⁹-: "If I don't get a week off, I will kill myself. That's all <3"

They come from us.

¹⁰harm: 1. please 2. please 3. please 4. please 5. please 6. please 7. please 8. please 9. please 10. Please

They come for us.

Here you lie below it all.

Accounting

Two gross total adults argue
about accounts receivable.

The decrease of 25%...
Equity? Not that...
Look at this table,
enlarge it, at the first
asset beginning
the animal year, follow
my index.

We are careful
at instruction
and instinct.

The baby is requiring
fixed attention.
Fix it.

Knife Fight

Kill yourselves. Here are the knives
I sharpen once a year.

Because the only fight worth fighting
is when you're armed.

Because you haven't done the dishes.
Because only the knives are clean unless

you want to scoop each other out
of this mess through your eyeballs?

Have a spoon. Blind yourselves.
Because I know more authentic

evils are invisible. Because I want
blind men in this house who can fight

with a fork. Because I want protection
and that means killing enthusiastically.

When your brother betrays your father,
I hope you think of me. I hope you thaw

the meat. And remember to turn off
all the lights at night. We are saving

electricity. We are saving the Earth.
Because if not, I will break all the recycled

bottles over your heads. There is something
to be done, and someone to clean up after you

unless I'm dead, and you leave the lights
flickering, and you leave knives in my memory

because you can't cook a meal
and you have let me down into hell

hungry.

I. HONOR STUDENT

Either way,
I know you
can take it
in the ass
or in the generous
mouth. Hard
direction
and soft
-hearted
construction.
Swallowing
each test
like a goat
without fear.
Milked for milk
in a sealed bottle.
Handling it
like a joystick,
a written essay,
a bidet with all
the pressure
plumbed
into you
like a pipe
bomb.

[Altar boy]

> "Shut away from men; they split
> into a thousand forms of evil...
> A brood forever opposing the Lord's
> Will, and again and again defeated."
> —Beowulf tr. Burton Raffel

Altar boy I was the opposite of, I knew
which words angered God. Owned it.
Discarded it. I still watched you over me.
Your frock ends at my heart. A reading

of unmoving bodies as verse from
the book of Desire. The salt pillars
of Sodom remain swayed but silent.
Gethsamane is so far away; the place of agony

isn't here. Circled around us
are masoned stoups with smoothed
angelic boys. My parents dip their fingers
in their cups; crucify their tears across their body.

Confirmation would soon arrive and polish
our bruises into peculiar stone. Curious
and devoted are we to our cause. The columns
in our legs wind up close to heaven, move

our foundations to shake the sanctus bells.
God is coming to consecrate. Boy, I feel the run

in my feet. Boy, I want Sunday for myself. Boy,
I wonder what shoes you're wearing,

how you take them off.

II. HONOR STUDENT

Far up front is where you're supposed to be. Up against the wall. A zillion years ago somebody spit in their hand, held it to a wall and then never let go. We preserved that fact as we do our mummies. This accelerated program ripens only those I hand pick. Remember, those in your year remain when you graduate. Every harvest, the apple falls so far away from the tree. You end up so sweet. Your mommy and daddy have so much apples in their eyes they could cry over the moon. You're so over the moon when you cry sometimes. The homerun being hit, never ever cried. You can hit the ground running, yknow? You will own so much earth when you land on your feet. You can run most distances into the ground if you just wanna go home.

Dead Boys Make The Best Men

For Dustin

Because they make the least noise.
A life of noise being turned off—
That's how I knew the first boy in my life
to die. His jokes, non-sequitur. He debates.
He talks about dirt being a whole meal.
It's a talking point. I love his speech
and how he's a boy of his word.
He becomes the dirt. Now, he's a man
of his silence.
In conclusion, he says and you see a full boy
eclipse. In the classroom, we let the movie
run with its life and when it ended, when everyone
stood up, I gazed at the projector glinting
with oil where he had no hair. You take hoodies for granted,
how he never pulled the hood up. He wore a mask
that he took off because he knew his illness.
He lived with his eyes. At lunch, he used his mouth
then never again.
You understand how absences are counted—
You write who you are in a record book.
Brand new blue, wonder who else it asks for answers.
Watch his only sibling become an only child.
Wonder how it goes. There is hot water and instant coffee
out of pocket. There are flower wreaths
that will be eaten by the wind. Even here,
there is magic and starving mages.
There are windows that face the graveyard.
There are names in the distance. His is laser-engraved,

we have a chance to trace it with our fingers
near the crematorium. Forget the fire for now.
Being in the same room makes prayer confident
like him. I tell him in private to be ready for us
to swarm him like sharks in a prayer circle.
At times, I admit we're following your blood
to school. At times, I let the worst alcohol spill over
our cups, hit our best shoes, strip the paint
from the gymnasium. All the men attended
our final game of the school year, our jerseys
were just right for our names to be cheered
from the bleachers or the sky, as far as anyone
was concerned when we left our classes to pick a fight
where we lived best. Where we couldn't reach
the ceiling, we climbed the scaffolds,
pulled intramural angels like you
down to earth from last year's championship.
Without a word, somebody broke the scoreboard
with how hard he threw the ball through his grief.
Without a word, we owned the court
with our fear.
Without a word, everyone wrote your name
on their shoes: midsoles, mudguards,
outsoles, toeboxes, laces, tongues.
We ran the full length of our lives
and screamed your name like the name
of our team at half-time.
I'm having fun, writing to you about
how we're winning, how we know
we're winning.

Lucky Me Pancit Canton

What is instant
is local and lovable
not beloved, just bled
into the bowl rimmed
with what will not last
the week, but perhaps
the year and days past
celebration.

Acknowledgements

Thank you FlowerSong Press for the paper, process, and patience you've given my work.

Thank you Malate Literary Folio, especially my poetry editor, Faith De Vega, for the faith and guidance behind the scenes.

Thank you to my fellow poets under Malate's poetry section for being irrepressible nuggets of joy.

Thank you Sir Ayer, Sir Vijae, and Carlo for your votes of confidence and words of wisdom which clothe this chapbook.

Thank you Rom for gracing this book's cover with your indelible art.

Many thanks to my professors, friends, and family for the boy they raised.

Thank you, Dustin, for Dustin.

About the Author

Rigel Portales is a 19-year-old Filipino poet afraid of disappearing. Fortunately, his works have appeared/are soon to appear on Cha, Palette Poetry, and Storm Cellar among other places. *DEAD BOYS MAKE THE BEST MEN* is his first published collection of work. He's currently a poetry staffer at the Malate Literary Folio. You can find him on his Twitter account @rijwrites where he writes to preserve and preserves to write. Given the chance, he wants to cook dinner for all his friends, all their favorite dishes, altogether. He also wants many things to outlive him.

FLOWERSONG
PRESS

FlowerSong Press nurtures essential verse
from, about, and throughout the
borderlands. Literary. Lyrical. Boundless.

Sign up for announcements about
new and upcoming titles at:

www.flowersongpress.com

www.ingramcontent.com/pod-product-compliance
Lightning Source LLC
Chambersburg PA
CBHW051650120626
46551CB00015B/2303